Sailing Ancient Seas

Harcourt
SCHOOL PUBLISHERS

Visit *The Learning Site!* www.harcourtschool.com

Greeks and the Sea

The country we now call Greece is mostly located on a peninsula surrounded by water. But nearly 2,000 islands are scattered around this rocky mainland. Because of this geography, ancient Greek life was tied to the sea. Much of an ancient Greek's food, such as fish, octopus, and squid, came from the ocean.

Most Greek cities were built near natural harbors where boats could anchor, safe from the dangerous tides and winds of the open sea. Foreign ships sailed into these busy harbors, carrying goods to trade with the Greek people.

The importance of the ocean is reflected in Greek mythology and literature. Poseidon, the god of the sea, was one of the three most powerful deities in the Greek religion. The Greeks built large temples to Poseidon and made offerings to him before undertaking sea journeys. They prayed that he would protect them from dangerous sailing conditions, pirates, and shipwrecks.

Poseidon

Greece

MACEDONIA
BULGARIA
Kavalla
ITALY
ALBANIA
Thessaloniki
Corfu
Larisa
Volos
GREECE
Ionian Sea
Euboea
Aegean Sea
TURKEY
N
W E
S
Corinth
Athens
Sparta
0   50   100 Miles
0   50   100 Kilometers
Mediterranean Sea
Rhodes
Crete

Greek myths told of sea dangers like Scylla and Charybdis.

Seafaring was often the subject of ancient Greek literature. Being a skilled sailor was a mark of a hero in Greek stories. The *Odyssey* tells the story of Odysseus, who angered the god Poseidon. He was forced to sail around the Mediterranean, lost, for 20 years before he could return home to Ithaca.

On his trip, Odysseus encountered many mythical sea dangers. Scylla, a many-headed monster, plucked sailors out of their ships. The monster Charybdis sucked water to create a giant whirlpool from which no ship could escape. Odysseus faced many dangers, but his abilities as a sailor and Poseidon's forgiveness finally brought him safely home.

Another Greek epic tells of the Greek hero Jason. He was sent by the gods on a quest to capture a sheep with a golden fleece. Jason sailed on a ship called the *Argo.* His route forced him to sail through the Wandering Rocks—two huge boulders that crashed together and destroyed ships. Jason tricked the rocks by sending a bird through first. The *Argo* slipped by just as the rocks reopened.

Business on the Sea

The ancient Greeks told myths about the ocean because the sea was central to their lives. Many Greeks made their living as fishers. Most fishers would sail only a short distance from the shore. Fish were more abundant farther out to sea. But it was much more risky for boats to sail there.

Greek fishers used long lines and bronze hooks or nets to fish. Once the fish were caught, most of them were salted. Salted fish lasted much longer than fresh fish, and could be transported inland and sold.

Fish were so important to the ancient Greeks that they took on religious meaning. Some religious groups forbade their followers to eat certain types of fish. At one Greek temple, visitors would throw fish into a pool. A priest would watch how the fish moved, and use these observations to predict each person's fortune.

This vase shows ancient Greeks fishing.

Different kinds of sea life decorate this Greek plate.

Traders and Merchants

The ancient world had a complex system of trade. Merchant ships sailed across the Mediterranean. Merchants would buy pottery, olive oil, and silver in Greece and transport them to other ports around the Mediterranean. In this way, the Greeks were able to trade for products like wood from the Middle East and grain from Egypt. Timber and wheat were not as plentiful in ancient Greece, and Greek goods were in high demand in other parts of the world.

Many of the goods transported on ships were stored in special clay jars called amphorae. An amphora was very large and shaped like a pear, with two round handles near the neck and a pointy bottom. An amphora could not stand up by itself. Amphorae were designed to be wedged in the bottom of a ship, where they served as ballast to help balance the boat. Each amphora was stamped with a picture and the name of the place where it came from, so sailors and merchants would know its origin.

Amphora

The Wreck at Ulu Burun

In 1984, at Ulu Burun, near the coast of Turkey, archaeologists discovered the wreck of an ancient trading ship. Archaeologists dove 150 feet to the wreck to investigate its cargo. Many amphorae have been recovered, though it is hard to tell what they contained because they have been underwater for thousands of years. Archaeologists also found pieces of copper and tin, which can be melted together to make bronze—the material for weapons and armor.

Navigating the Ancient Seas

The Greeks were not the only skilled sailors in the Mediterranean. In fact, the most legendary sailors in the ancient world were a people called the Phoenicians. They lived on the coasts of what are now Lebanon and Israel.

The Phoenicians were expert shipbuilders, using cedar trees from Lebanon. Their sailors were so skilled that other countries hired the Phoenician navy to fight for them. The Phoenicians pioneered trading between cities on the Mediterranean. Historians believe they carried their alphabet to the Greeks through trade. The Phoenician alphabet is the basis of the alphabet we use today.

The Dangers of the Sea

No matter how skilled the sailor, sailing in the ancient world was very difficult. The ancient Greeks had no devices to help them navigate. Once under sail, they often could not tell where they were.

Sailors had some ability to use the moon and the stars to navigate at night, but most sailing was done during the day. It took many years for Greek thinkers to create navigational charts and devices to help determine a ship's exact location on the sea.

Greek ships tried to stay within sight of the coast.

For the most part, ancient sailors made certain that they could always see the coast. This made long-distance voyages very time-consuming. Sometimes sailors would sail across the open water, but this was a dangerous thing to do. The ships were not sturdy, and it was risky to sail them in storms.

Sailing season, between spring and fall, was considered the safest time for voyages because there were fewer storms and more favorable winds. Few sailors were brave enough to sail during the treacherous winter months.

The ancient Greeks believed that gods controlled storms on the ocean.

Large sails powered the merchant ships that made long voyages. The ships also had rowers who pulled oars when the wind was still. The ships were steered by two large oars attached to the stern, or back, of the boat. Each ship would be loaded with amphorae, as well as pottery and other products. When it was time to stop for the night, ships would drop huge stone anchors.

Ancient Greek anchor

Mapping the World

The first map of the world is said to have been created by a philosopher named Anaximander. It was made out of bronze and showed all the known world. Anaximander's map has disappeared, so scholars are not certain if this map actually existed. But many stories are told about it in ancient Greek writing.

In the second century A.D., Ptolemy, another Greek, wrote the first instructions for drawing a map of the world. Ptolemy's map was based on longitude and latitude, and may have been the first map designed using mathematical calculations.

However, Ptolemy's map was also based on unscientific reports from travelers. Much of it was wrong. The map showed Africa and China connected to each other, making the Indian Ocean into one giant lake. Ptolemy's instructions for making a world map were used for centuries. His ideas allowed Greeks in the ancient world to understand where they lived in relation to the rest of the known world.

The Tower of the Winds in Athens, Greece

Navigational Tools

As time went on, other navigational tools were invented and used by ancient Greeks. An astronomer named Hipparchus may have invented the astrolabe. The astrolabe is a device that allows people to determine their longitude from the position of the stars and the time of night. Using this device, sailors would know how far east or west they had traveled. With navigational instruments, it became easier for sailors to find their way around the ocean.

Astrolabe

Another important factor in navigation is the wind. The Tower of the Winds is an ancient building that still stands in Athens, Greece. It shows sculptures of the eight wind gods the Greeks worshipped. Each wind direction is represented by a god with a distinct personality. Zephyrus, the west wind, was a lucky wind who helped sailors reach their destination. But other winds, like Notus, the south wind, brought storms. These wind gods were thought to be unlucky.

Ancient Greek Explorers

Sailing vast distances took years and could be very dangerous. But some Greek explorers were said to have braved these journeys and sailed all over the world. Scholars have trouble determining if these ancient voyages were actually made. All that survives of the explorers' journeys are descriptions in books by ancient authors. Even in the ancient world, these tales were doubted. At the time, there was very little evidence to support the explorers' fantastic claims.

Pytheas

One of these explorers was a man named Pytheas, who lived on the southern coast of what is now France. His reports tell of a voyage into the Atlantic Ocean, all the way around present-day Britain.

After he had explored this area, he claims to have sailed even farther north. Some historians believe he may have sailed as far as the Arctic Ocean. In his writings, he described a night that lasted only two or three hours and an ocean filled with ice.

Possible Route of Pytheas

— Outbound
— Inbound

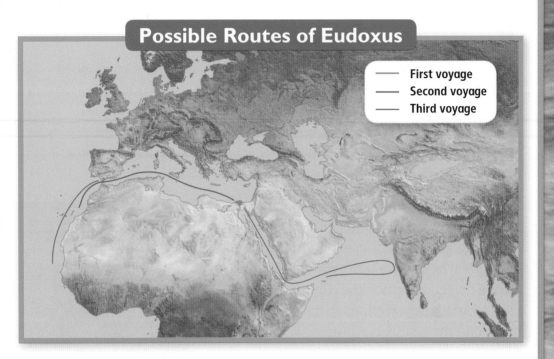

Possible Routes of Eudoxus

- First voyage
- Second voyage
- Third voyage

Eudoxus of Cyzicus

Another story tells of Eudoxus of Cyzicus, who lived in Egypt. He was sent by the Egyptian king on an expedition across the Indian Ocean. Eudoxus survived the voyage to India and returned to Egypt with a ship full of exotic Indian objects. The Egyptian king took all his cargo.

After this setback, Eudoxus decided to find an alternate route to India that avoided sailing past Egypt. His goal was to bring back valuable merchandise from India and sell it himself. He planned to sail west out of the Mediterranean Sea and then all the way around Africa. On his first attempt, reports say he was forced to turn around south of Morocco. But he tried again.

He sailed down the west coast of Africa and was never heard from again. Perhaps he reached India safely and stayed there, or perhaps he was shipwrecked. No matter what happened to Eudoxus, he is thought to be one of the first explorers brave enough to attempt sailing around the continent of Africa.

Sailing into Battle

Sailors were vital to commerce, exploration, and war. Often, when leagues of Greek city-states fought, there would be spectacular sea battles. Navies were an essential part of most city-states' defenses. The Athenian navy was so powerful that it controlled most of the Mediterranean. Other cities paid Athens to use its navy for protection, and to make sure that Athens's navy never attacked them.

Why did Athens have the most powerful Greek navy? According to legend, the Athenians received a message from the oracle at Delphi. The Greeks believed that the god Apollo helped them see the future at Delphi. They would bring offerings to the sanctuary there, and the oracle, a priestess, would make a prophecy.

This piece of pottery shows a Greek warship.

When the leaders of Athens asked how the city could survive an attack by the invading Persians, the oracle answered that the city would be safe behind wooden walls. A powerful politician named Themistocles (thuh•MIS•tuh•kleez) interpreted the prophecy to mean that Athens should defend itself with the wooden walls of its ships.

Bow

Themistocles persuaded the citizens of Athens to spend all of their money on building warships and training their navy. When the Persians attacked, the Athenians who fought from behind the walls of the Acropolis were killed. But the Athenian navy survived and won a remarkable victory over the Persians.

Keel

Triremes

Greek navies fought with battleships called triremes. These ships had three levels. On each level sat many rowers. Each trireme was built by carving the keel, or bottom, of the boat, then adding ribs. Once the hull, or outside, of the boat was finished, the interior of the boat would be built, including benches for the oarsmen.

The triremes were not completely waterproof and could not be immersed in the sea for long periods of time. Each night they had to be dragged from the water to dry off. In the harbor of modern Athens, archaeologists have found long stone ramps that were used to drag the ships to dry land. At the end of each ramp was a large building, where the trireme would dry safely.

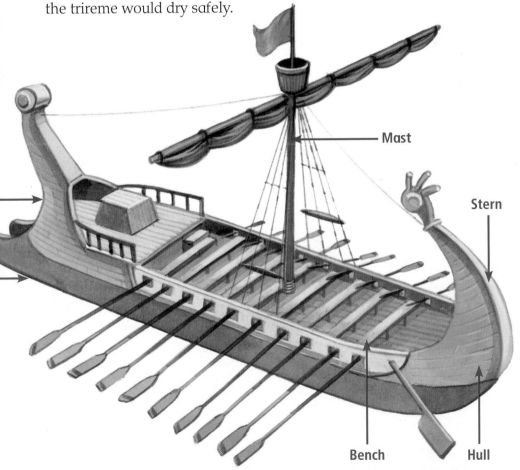

Mast

Stern

Bench

Hull

Sea Battles

Each trireme had a large bronze ram attached to the bow, or front, of the ship at the level of the water. In battle, triremes would try to ram each other and make a hole that would sink the other ship. A favorite battle tactic was to sail next to an enemy ship and use the ram to break all the oars on one side. With half of its oars missing, the boat could not move. The attacking trireme would then turn around and sail straight into the side of its opponent and make an enormous hole in the hull.

Once the ram was firmly in the side of a disabled ship, soldiers would jump from one ship to another. Many enemy sailors would leap from a rammed ship and try to swim to safety. In some conflicts, soldiers would wait on the beaches in sight of the sea battle and kill enemy sailors who tried to swim ashore.

In 480 B.C., Xerxes, the Persian emperor, led an expedition to conquer Greece. The Persian navy fought the Greek navy in a great battle. The Greek navy was vastly outnumbered. But it aggressively attacked the Persian fleet.

A sea battle between the Greeks and Persians

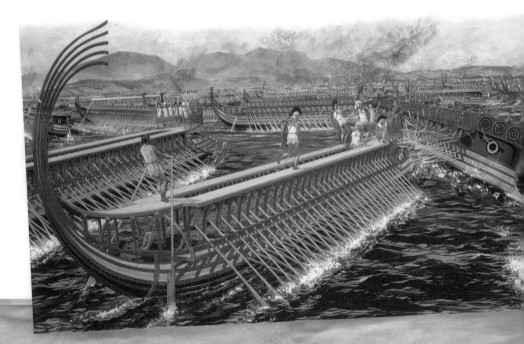

The sea has always been important to the Greek people.

The Greek ships formed a circle, with their bows facing out. The massive Persian fleet surrounded them. The Persians tried to attack the Greek boats but began crashing into each other instead. The smaller, faster Greek boats were able to sail around the confusion. In the end the Greeks retreated, but they learned many valuable lessons that day about naval combat.

The ancient Greeks depended on the sea for their survival. They fought wars and fished for food. They wrote stories about sea monsters and sailing heroes. They traveled to distant lands and learned about the world. The ancient seas were deeply important to the development of ancient Greece's economy and culture, and to the spread of Greek civilization across the ancient world.

Think and Respond

1. How is the sea reflected in Greek mythology and literature?

2. What caused ancient Greek sailors and fishers to stay close to shore?

3. Why were the first maps and navigational tools so important to ancient Greeks?

4. Why was the smaller Greek navy able to attack the larger Persian navy?

5. Why do you think the Greeks adopted the Phoenician alphabet?

 # Activity

With a few of your classmates, imagine that you are on a Greek ship sailing to explore uncharted waters. Where are you going? What sorts of things are you looking for? What will you see? Create a script for a radio play about your experiences.

Photo Credits
Front Cover AAAC/Topham/The Image Works; Background Border (throughout) PhotoDisc, Inc.; 2 Alinari/Art Resource, NY; 3 Erich Lessing/Art Resource, NY; 4 (t) Erich Lessing/Art Resource, NY, (b) Réunion des Musées Nationaux/Art Resource, NY; 5(t, b) Ina; 6 Private Collection, The Stapleton Collection/Bridgeman Art Library; 7 (t) Private Collection, The Stapleton Collection/Bridgeman Art Library, (b) Ina; 8-9 Sandro Vannini/Corbis; 9 Bibliotheque Nationale de Cartes et Plans, Paris, France/Bridgeman Art Library; 10 Courtauld Institute of Art /Art and Architecture; 12 Erich Lessing/Art Resource, NY; 14 akg-images/Peter Connolly; 15 and Back Cover Digital Vision/Punch Stock.

Illustration Credits
2 Mapquest; 10, 11 Bill Melvin; 13 Doug Knutson.